TO: Grandma

FROM: Imani

12/25/15

Copyright © 2013 Hallmark Licensing, LLC

Published by Hallmark Gift Books,
a division of Hallmark Cards, Inc.,
Kansas City, MO 64141
Visit us on the Web at Hallmark.com.

All rights reserved. No part of this publication may be
reproduced, transmitted, or stored in any form or by
any means without the prior written permission of the
publisher.

Editorial Director: Delia Berrigan
Editor: Emily Osborn
Art Director: Jan Mastin
Designer: Mark Voss
Production Artist: Dan Horton

ISBN: 978-1-59530-636-4
BOK1299

Printed and bound in China

NOW YOU'RE 80!

BY BRANDON CROSE

 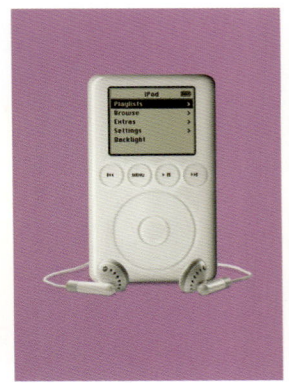 

Sandwiched between the more ostentatious greatest generation and the baby boomers, you're a proud member of the silent generation. And that's fine with you—your record speaks for itself. You were born during the worst years of the Great Depression, and your very first lessons were of self-sacrifice and civic duty. You've survived some of the hardest times this country has yet seen, as well as your grandchildren's fashion choices. From the Dirty Thirties all the way to today, the story of America's growth is actually your story, and that tale is far from over . . .

WHEN YOU WERE BORN

IN THE NEWS

Franklin Delano Roosevelt promised a New Deal for Americans beset with joblessness and poverty. Congress began approving FDR's relief programs, including the Works Progress Administration, which put millions of unemployed back to work.

With times so tough, crime made top headlines more days than not: the Lindbergh baby kidnapping, Bonnie and Clyde, and the exploits of public enemy No. 1, John Dillinger, were just a few of the more sensational stories your parents heard.

Advances in media technologies kept your parents informed of events around the world, such as Italy invading Ethiopia, Japan invading China, and Adolph Hitler naming himself führer of Germany.

Prohibition was at last repealed, and Coca-Cola sales dropped as many, perhaps even your parents and their neighbors, began enjoying drinks of a different nature . . .

"The only thing we have to fear is fear itself."

FDR

EVENTS

The Great Depression was at its peak: One in four workers was unemployed, and one in five children was not getting enough to eat. If your older siblings were not sent away to live with relatives, they were very likely responsible for bathing and dressing you in your early years. Everyone had to do his or her part.

As if times weren't hard enough, more than two hundred thousand families from plains states were forced to abandon their failing farms and migrate west to California. They were called "Okies" because many of them came from Oklahoma, where the Dust Bowl was most severe.

However, it wasn't all bad: after many protests and strikes, some even violent, the Wagner Act protected your father's (and, someday, your) right to organize in a labor union.

Amelia Earhart became the first person, male or female, to successfully pilot a transpacific course from Hawaii to California.

WHEN YOU WERE BORN

MUSIC

You may not remember now, but "On the Good Ship Lollipop" by Shirley Temple, "What a Diff'rence a Day Made" by the Dorsey Brothers, and "I'm in the Mood for Love" by Frances Langford were among the first songs you ever heard.

Woody Guthrie traveled around the country singing about the struggles many families faced, with songs like "The Great Dust Storm," "Dust Bowl Refugee," and "Brother, Can You Spare a Dime?"

Very few people could afford to go to a concert, but if your family had a radio, you could listen to all the music you wanted! Radio was so popular and widespread now that a new agency, the Federal Communications Commission (FCC), was created to regulate it.

In fact, it was probably through the radio that your family first heard the sounds of swing, big-band, and jazz music that would become so popular during your childhood.

MOVIES

If they could afford it, your parents may have taken an evening to see one of the popular movies of the time: *Cleopatra, The Gay Divorcee,* or *San Francisco.*

It Happened One Night swept the top five Academy Award categories, and the sight of best actor Clark Gable's bare chest caused a sharp decline in men's underwear sales.

While the Marx Brothers found great success with *A Night at the Opera,* science fiction films such as *Bride of Frankenstein* and *Flash Gordon* began to cause a stir.

Other silver-screen (and box-office) stars of the day included Will Rogers, Joan Crawford, Wallace Beery, Janet Gaynor, James Cagney, Mae West, Spencer Tracy, and Claudette Colbert.

But the biggest box-office star of them all was Shirley Temple, who starred in *Stand Up and Cheer!, Curly Top,* and *The Littlest Rebel.* She also became the youngest Oscar winner at the age of six.

TV & RADIO

By the time you were born, television was little more than a science experiment. However, there were about 19.2 million radios in American homes. In just a few years, that number would rise to forty-four million—four out of five homes had a radio.

And why not? Your parents could enjoy the comedic styles of Eddie Cantor, Jack Benny, and George Burns and Gracie Allen; detective shows like *The Adventures of Sam Spade* and *Yours Truly, Johnny Dollar;* and rollicking adventures such as *Buck Rogers in the Twenty-Fifth Century, The Lone Ranger,* and *Jack Armstrong, the All-American Boy.*

Perhaps your mother listened to popular "soap operas" (called so because they were frequently sponsored by soap companies like Oxydol) *Ma Perkins* and *The Romance of Helen Trent.* Long-running soap opera *The Guiding Light* also got its start as a radio serial during this time.

The invention of frequency-modulated (FM) radio allowed for a more clear, static-free signal than the amplitude-modulated (AM) signal your parents were used to. And a good thing, too—from FDR's "fireside chats" to *The March of Time,* the radio had become your parents' best and most reliable source of news.

"When I was a boy, the Dead Sea was only sick."

GEORGE BURNS

SPORTS

Two now-familiar football teams were also born during this time: the Philadelphia Eagles and Pittsburgh Steelers both entered the National Football League. The popularity of college football necessitated more bowls than just the Rose. The Orange, Sun, Sugar, and Cotton bowls were added to the yearly lineup.

Though the American League won the second Major League Baseball All-Star Game, left-handed pitcher Carl Hubbell of the National League set a new record by consecutively striking out George Herman "Babe" Ruth, Lou Gehrig, Jimmie Foxx, Al Simmons, and Joe Cronin.

Babe Ruth later went on to hit a six-hundred-foot home run against the Pittsburgh Pirates—his 714th, a record that would stand unbroken for thirty-nine years.

American running and jumping superstar Jesse Owens won a victory against Aryan supremacy when he scored four gold medals in the 1936 Summer Olympics in Berlin, humiliating Adolf Hitler. In fact, of the ten African Americans who participated that year, nine won gold medals.

POP CULTURE

....

For baby boys, your parents were most likely to name you Robert, James, John, William, or Richard. For baby girls, Mary, Barbara, Shirley, Betty, and Dorothy were the most popular choices.

Many of your favorite comic strip characters—Tarzan, Little Orphan Annie, Dick Tracy, Terry and the Pirates, Buck Rogers, Li'l Abner, Flash Gordon and, of course, Superman—were all born with you.

Seeking an escape from the hard financial realities of the time, many chose to pass "Go" and collect $200. Monopoly hit the shelves and immediately sold twenty million sets in one week.

The average annual salary was less than $1,400. A newspaper cost $0.05, and a quart of milk was $0.10. If they could afford it, a new Chevrolet might have cost your parents anywhere from $465 to $695.

WHEN YOU WERE
A KID

IN THE NEWS

"A day of infamy" silenced all but the most stalwart proponents of the America First antiwar movement. An early morning Japanese air assault on the US military base in Pearl Harbor damaged or destroyed 21 ships and 341 aircraft and killed 2,403 Americans. "Remember Pearl Harbor" became the rallying cry for America's entry into World War II.

On presidential order, more than 110,000 Japanese Americans were relocated to one of ten internment camps, where they endured overcrowded and poor living conditions for two and a half years.

After receiving a troubling telegram from Switzerland, the American Jewish Congress began holding rallies in major US cities to raise awareness of the rumored "Nazi death camps." The Jewish death toll was thought to exceed three million people . . . the final number was twice that.

The massive D-Day invasion at Normandy, France, involved more than 150,000 soldiers, nearly 7,000 ships, and just over 15,000 aircraft. Victory had a steep cost—by the end of the first day, an estimated 10,000 Allied soldiers were either dead or wounded.

A Day of Infamy

ATTACK ON PEARL HARBOR

EVENTS

It was a time of sweeping change: inspired by "Rosie the Riveter," several million women excelled at jobs that were traditionally male-only, helping to build the ships, tanks, planes, and guns that were needed to win the war.

For the first time, women were also allowed to join the four military branches as auxiliary support. More than three hundred thousand volunteered to become "soldiers in skirts"—SPARS, WASP WAC, and WAVES.

Everyday Americans banded together like never before—even kids like you! From collecting millions of tons of scrap rubber and metals to donating every spare cent to buy a total of $135 billion in war bonds, everyone did his or her part to support the war effort.

Though Sir Alexander Fleming accidentally discovered penicillin years before you were born, scientists at last successfully used the mold-based medicine to stop a bacterial infection . . . just in time to begin treating the many wounded soldiers abroad.

MUSIC

Some of your favorite songs might have included "Boogie Woogie Bugle Boy" by the Andrews Sisters, "White Christmas" by Bing Crosby, and "Paper Doll" by the Mills Brothers.

Perhaps you listened to the *Grand Ole Opry* or Gene Autry's *Melody Ranch* on your family's radio or—if you were extremely fortunate—your very own brand-new Zenith portable or RCA Victor personal radio (with genuine leather carrying case)!

Dmitri Shostakovich's Symphony no. 7, written about the horrors of war Shostakovich witnessed in Leningrad, found a sympathetic worldwide audience, while the Allies adopted Beethoven's Fifth Symphony as their unofficial victory theme. (The first four notes happen to be Morse code for the letter "V.")

Big bands were still a big deal, with Tommy and Jimmy Dorsey, Harry James, Artie Shaw, Duke Ellington, Benny Goodman, and Glenn Miller all selling top records.

WHEN YOU WERE A KID

MOVIES

You may have been too young to remember seeing Walt Disney's first feature-length cartoon, *Snow White and the Seven Dwarfs,* but you might remember seeing his follow-up films *Pinocchio, Dumbo, Fantasia,* and *Bambi* when they were first in the theaters.

Adapted from the John Steinbeck novel, *The Grapes of Wrath* depicted the California migration that many families endured, possibly including yours. The movie won two Academy Awards for best director and best supporting actress.

While Hollywood "went to war," many famous actors did actually go to war, including James Stewart, Frank Capra, Mickey Rooney, and Clark Gable.

A movie ticket was only a quarter, and admission got you two movies, newsreels of the war, an episode of a weekly serial such as *Dick Tracy vs. Crime Inc.* or *Jungle Girl,* and a cartoon. Donald Duck starred in many of the cartoons, but his most famous was the anti-Nazi *Der Fuehrer's Face,* which won an Academy Award for best short feature.

TV & RADIO

Like refrigerators and stoves, the production of new television sets was banned during the war, so they were difficult to find and expensive—a staggering $700!

Radio remained king, and your family's standards probably still included FDR's "fireside chats" as well as the *Lux Radio Theater; Ma Perkins; The Shadow; Fibber McGee and Molly, Gang Busters;* and *Sherlock Holmes* starring Basil Rathbone.

"Soaps" remained the most popular daytime radio programs, with *The Guiding Light, Woman in White, The Road of Life,* and *The Right to Happiness* leading the pack. You may not have known this, but one woman—Irna Phillips—wrote all of these.

Many future television stars had successful radio shows during this time, such as Milton Berle, Jack Benny, Abbott and Costello, and Red Skelton.

NBC became the first commercial TV station, and the first-ever commercial was for the Bulova Time Signal watch.

SPORTS

From an inauspicious start to underdog hero of the Great Depression, the thoroughbred Seabiscuit won the $121,000 Santa Anita Handicap in the final race of his long career.

Joe "The Brown Bomber" Louis successfully defended the heavyweight title against twenty-five contenders before enlisting as a private in the US Army. The heavyweight title was frozen until his return.

Over 1,000 of America's baseball heroes also went to war after the bombing of Pearl Harbor—including "The Yankee Clipper" himself, Joe Dimaggio . . . but not before he hit in a record fifty-six straight games!

With many of baseball fans' favorite players gone, sports enthusiasts turned to college football. The 1942 Rose Bowl, typically held in Pasadena, California, was instead relocated to Durham, North Carolina, for fear of another Japanese attack. Despite the unexpected home advantage, Duke still lost to Oregon State, 20-16.

POP CULTURE

With so many materials going to the war effort, your childhood was likely not littered with fancy toys. Old classics such as Tinkertoys, Lincoln Logs, and Erector Sets were still around, but you also enjoyed playing with your siblings or other neighborhood kids in games of jump rope, hopscotch, hide-and-seek, red light-green light, red rover, or marbles.

Donald Duck was not the only cartoon to go to war: Theodor Seuss Geisel (later known as "Dr. Seuss") contributed numerous political cartoons and animated training videos to the cause, and Captain America's very first comic featured the red, white, and blue superhero punching Adolf Hitler in the face!

In your grocery store, Kellogg's Raisin Bran made its debut, while Cheeri O'Leary introduced CheeriOats as "The Breakfast Food You've Always Wanted!" (Its name would later shorten to the now-familiar Cheerios.)

Richard and Maurice McDonald opened the first McDonald's restaurant in San Bernardino, California.

WHEN YOU WERE
A TEENAGER

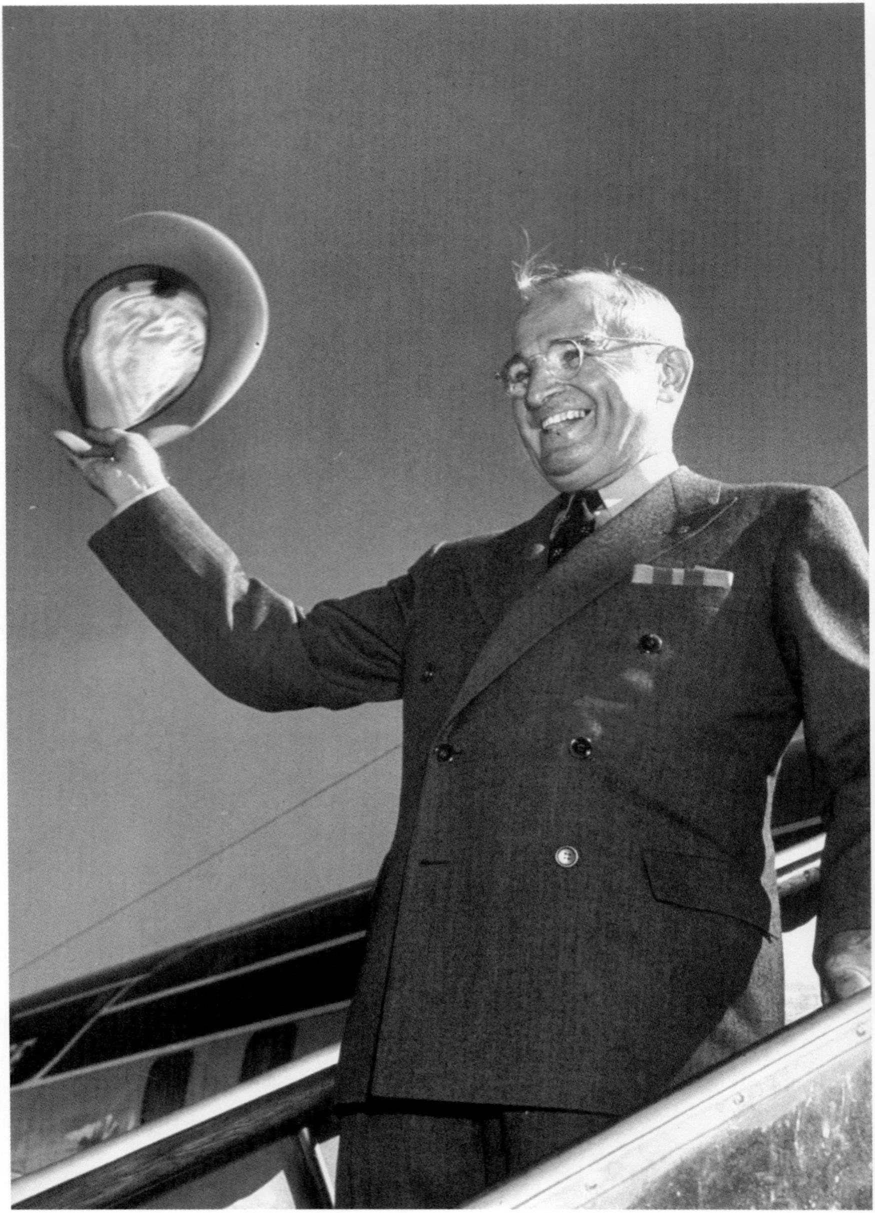

IN THE NEWS

If you read the *Chicago Tribune*, you probably thought that Thomas Dewey beat Harry Truman in the 1948 presidential election. The issue went to press on November 3rd before all the results were in—Truman, of course, was the victor.

Having lived through World War II, you now watched as the less popular Korean War claimed 36,940 American and 3.9 million Korean lives.

You may have been among the seven million people who attended the New York City ticker-tape parade thrown for military legend General Douglas MacArthur after his dismissal from duty by President Truman.

It was a time of prosperity and material comfort, but the Red Scare was in full effect: Ethel and Julius Rosenberg were sentenced to death by electric chair for sharing US nuclear secrets with the Soviet Union. (Ethel's brother was the prosecution's chief witness.)

EVENTS

. . . .

The invention of the atomic bomb and the subsequent annihilation of two Japanese cities, Hiroshima and Nagasaki, definitively ended the war and gave birth to an atomic age of boundless scientific achievement. Suddenly, anything was possible . . . even the end of the world.

More than 1.5 million African Americans had served in the war, and many had been promoted to officer ranks. Long-held racial divisions were breaking down, and in 1948, President Truman ordered the desegregation of the armed forces.

Two-thirds of American homes had a telephone, and AT&T had just introduced direct-dial coast-to-coast telephone service. The first call was from New Jersey to California and took eighteen seconds to connect.

The first commercial computer, the UNIVersal Automatic Computer (UNIVAC I), had just hit "shelves"—but at fourteen by seven by nine feet, it took up most of a room.

WHEN YOU WERE A TEENAGER

Please
Answer
Promptly
DEF
ABC
GHI
JKL
MNO
PRS
TUV
WXY
Z
OPERATOR

Gene Autry's perennial holiday favorite "Rudolph the Red-Nosed Reindeer" hit the airwaves for the first time.

MUSIC

Jazz and bebop were still big. After performing with other legends such as Dizzy Gillespie, Miles Davis, and Fats Navarro, Billy Eckstine became a tremendously popular solo artist, rivaling even Frank Sinatra with hits like "Everything I Have is Yours" and "I Apologize."

Perhaps you held hands with your sweetheart and listened to Jackie Gleason's first album, *Music for Lovers Only*—it remained on the top ten charts for a record 153 weeks.

Other hit songs you listened to (perhaps on a 45 rpm vinyl disc or new transistor radio) included "Let's Take an Old-Fashioned Walk" by Frank Sinatra and Doris Day, "Mona Lisa" by Nat King Cole, and "Hello, Young Lovers" by Perry Como.

MOVIES

Some of the big movies of your teenage years—including *The Third Man, Sunset Boulevard,* and *All About Eve*—are still classics today.

You may have also seen *A Streetcar Named Desire*, starring Marlon Brando and Vivien Leigh. It was nominated for twelve Academy Awards and won four of them, losing best actor to Humphrey Bogart in *The African Queen.*

Cold War fear of world annihilation found its way into many movies of the time, but none so explicitly as in the science fiction hit *The Day the Earth Stood Still.*

The Red Scare that would soon sweep the nation began with hearings by the House Un-American Activities Committee, which led to the blacklisting of some of Hollywood's greatest talents, such as Charlie Chaplin, Lillian Hellman, Arthur Miller, Orson Welles, and Dorothy Parker, who famously wrote in a letter to the committee: "I cannot and will not cut my conscience to fit this year's fashions."

TV

After the war, a movie producer predicted, "Television won't be able to hold on to any market it captures after the first six months. People will soon get tired of staring at a plywood box every night." How wrong he was—American families turned from radio to TV in greater numbers with each passing year.

Some of your favorite shows may have included *The Original Amateur Hour, Texaco Star Theater, Toast of the Town* with Ed Sullivan, *Candid Camera, Studio One, The Philco Television Playhouse, Arthur Godfrey and His Friends,* and *Your Show of Shows.*

You witnessed many now-familiar firsts. The wildly popular Milton Berle (or "Uncle Miltie") hosted the first telethon, raising one million dollars for cancer research in fourteen hours.

You also saw the first television broadcast of a World Series—the New York Yankees vs. the Brooklyn Dodgers.

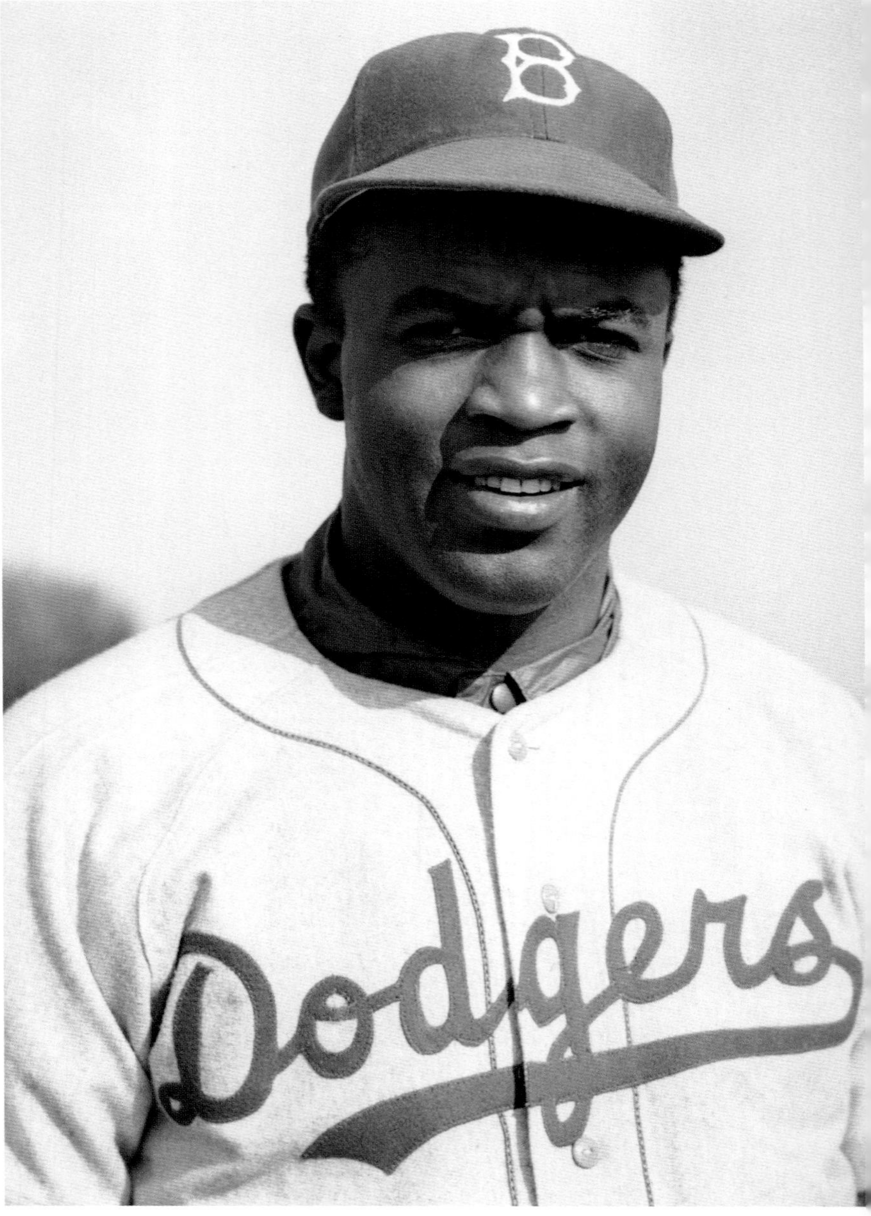
B
Dodgers

SPORTS

· ·

The Games of the XIV Olympiad (or, less formally, the 1948 Summer Olympics in London) were only the second of your lifetime—because of the outbreak of war they had been suspended since the 1936 Summer Olympics in Berlin. The United States dominated with seventy-six medals, forty of them gold.

The National Basketball Association (NBA) grew out of the Basketball Association of America (BAA), with six-foot-ten-inch George Mikan easily dominating those early games.

Did you hear "the shot heard round the world"? In the bottom of the ninth, Bobby Thomson hit a spectacular three-run home run, winning the National League pennant for the New York Giants.

Jackie Robinson broke professional baseball's color barrier by becoming the first African American to play Major League Baseball since 1889 and then made history again by earning Rookie of the Year his first season.

POP CULTURE

The term "teen-ager" was first used to describe you and your friends. With the war over and the economy beginning to boom, a true youth culture started to emerge: this meant more spending money for buying the clothes and music you liked, more time for varsity sports and slumber parties, the freedom to begin dating, and maybe, eventually, college!

During the war, you had to be on a list to buy a car, but now new models were everywhere. If you bought or were given your first car around this time, it might have been a 1948 Buick Roadmaster, 1949 Cadillac Series 62, 1950 Pontiac Chieftain, or a 1951 Ford Crown Victoria two-door hardtop (with optional Ford-O-Matic automatic transmission!).

Meat was still expensive, and the dollar didn't go as far, but one thing wasn't in short supply for long: new homes! Suburbia was born with the rapid creation of developments, such as Levittown, New York, a community of seventeen thousand newly built (and nearly identical) homes, where grass had to be cut once a week and laundry hung on rotary racks.

Silly Putty is "invented" during the war when a General Electric engineer tried to create a synthetic rubber.

**WHEN YOU WERE
IN YOUR 20s**

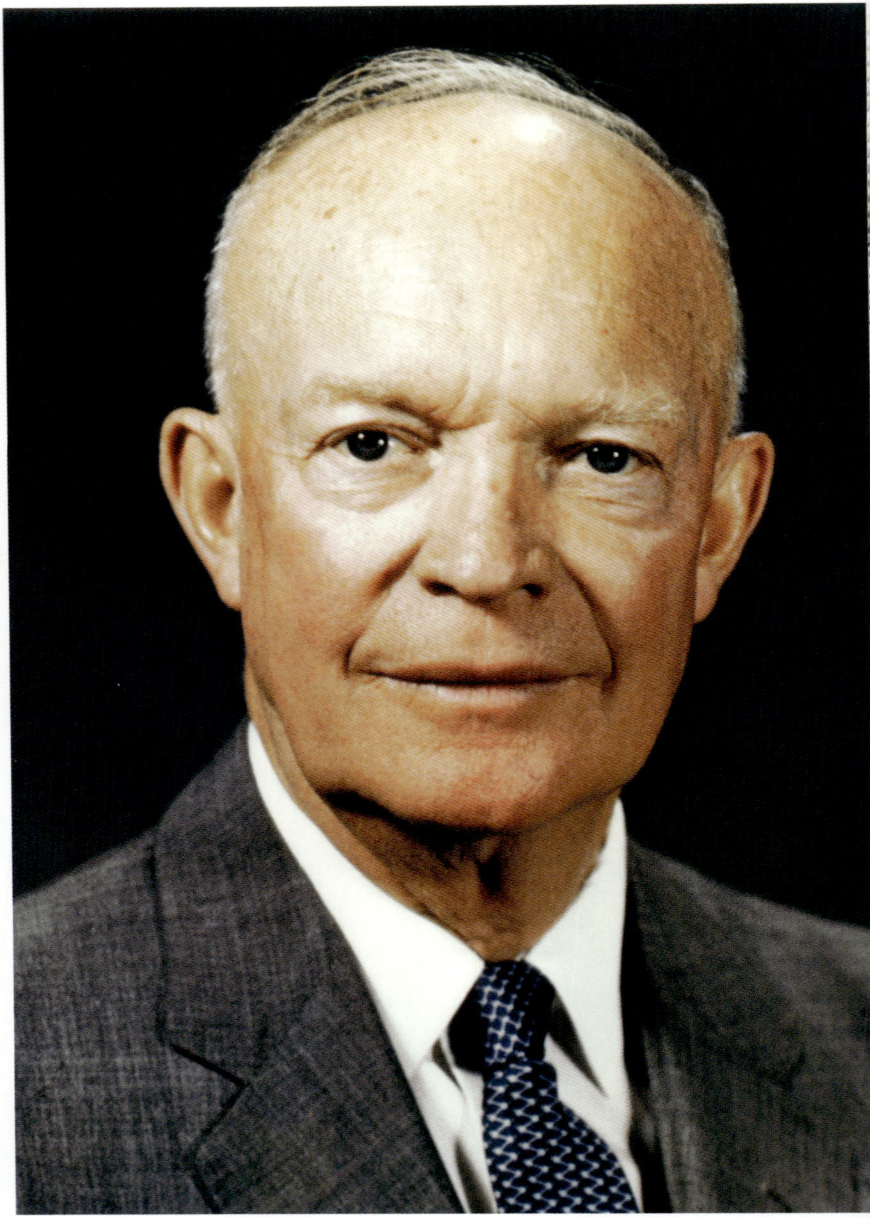

IN THE NEWS

After tens of thousands of East German refugees fled to West Berlin to escape communist rule, the German Democratic Republic erected a wire fence to divide East Berlin from West Berlin. This simple fence would later become an eleven-foot concrete barrier known as the Berlin Wall.

You still liked Ike: after a spate of health problems, President Eisenhower barely campaigned for his second term and handily won over Adlai Stevenson— 36 million votes to 26 million.

In Alabama, racial violence raged: Freedom Riders were savagely beaten by white mobs in Birmingham, and martial law was declared in Montgomery after a crowd of both adults and children began throwing stones through the windows of a church where Dr. Martin Luther King Jr. was speaking.

EVENTS

Scientific advancements seemed to belong more to science fiction than reality: Sputnik I and then II circled the earth, NASA was born with the passing of The National Aeronautics and Space Act, and an early test of the hydrogen bomb at Bikini Atoll was estimated to burn five times hotter than the sun's core.

Alan B. Shepard became the first American in space—his flight lasted fifteen minutes. Later, a chimpanzee named Enos circled the earth twice for three hours and twenty-one minutes.

The modern environmental movement was born: Rachel Carson's book *Silent Spring* warned (among other things) that the widespread use of DDT and other insecticides was exposing us to over five hundred different chemicals.

The world became a smaller place with the invention of the jet engine. Pan American's jet planes offered America's first commercial transatlantic flights: New York to London.

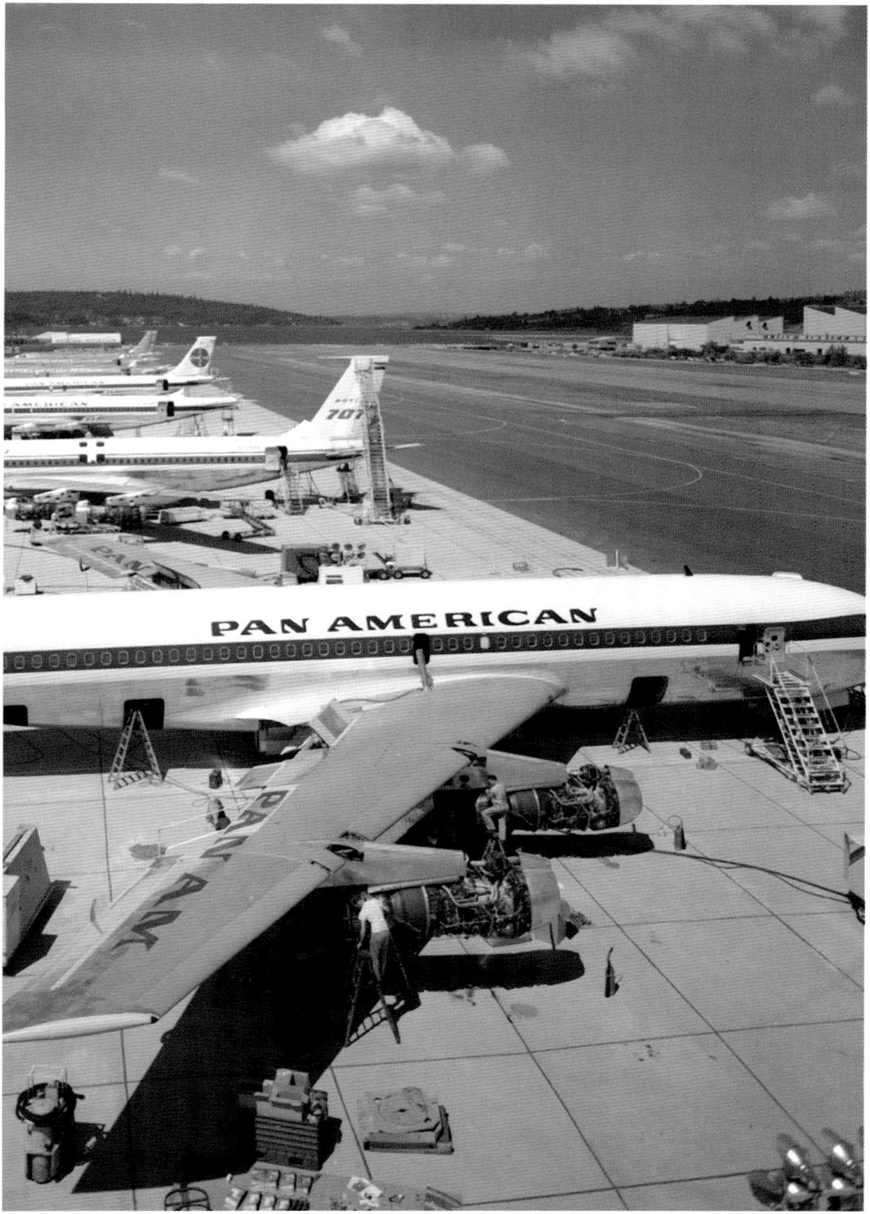
PAN AMERICAN
707

Buddy Holly, Richie Valens, and JP "The Big Bopper" Richardson met their end in a tragic plane crash.

MUSIC

Add an electric guitar to rhythm and blues, and you have rock 'n' roll—the sound of your early twenties. Your stars included Little Richard, Jerry Lee Lewis, Bill Haley and His Comets, and the King of Rock 'n' Roll himself: Elvis Presley, with his hit songs "Hound Dog," "Love Me Tender," and "Heartbreak Hotel."

Other familiar songs included Frank Sinatra's "All the Way," Peggy Lee's "Fever," and Dinah Washington's "What a Diff'rence a Day Makes."

You had probably never heard of The Pendletones, but you listened up when the band changed its name to The Beach Boys—"Surfin' Safari" and "Surfin' USA" were top twenty hits.

MOVIES

. . . .

Drive-in theaters were popping up everywhere—two movies for the price of one was a good deal, too, if you could put up with all the high school kids!

You might have taken an evening to see *The Ten Commandments, Around the World in Eighty Days,* or *Peyton Place* with your college sweetheart or new spouse.

After three marriages and many movies, larger-than-life actress Marilyn Monroe died from an overdose of sleeping pills in her home at the age of 36.

An Affair to Remember and *Cleopatra* were both highly successful remakes of movies that first came out when you were very young. This would certainly not be the last time Hollywood did this . . .

DRIVE·IN THEATER

BEN-HUR

TV

By the mid-50s, Americans were buying an average of seven million TV sets per year. Approximately one in seven American families owned at least one television, and the typical viewer spent forty-two hours per week watching it.

You may have enjoyed convenient and modern Swanson TV dinners on folding TV tables while watching shows, such as *The Red Skelton Hour, I Love Lucy, Gunsmoke, General Electric Theater, American Bandstand,* and *The $64,000 Question.*

You may have even been one of the thirty million viewers to watch the wedding of celebrity actress Grace Kelly to Prince Rainier III of Monaco.

Quiz show scandals and payola investigations prompted FCC Chairmain Newton N. Minow to call television "a vast wasteland." Years later, the *SS Minnow* in *Gilligan's Island* was sarcastically named in Minow's honor.

SPORTS

Mickey Mantle's hallowed Triple Crown season included .340 batting and fifty-two home runs, helping the Yankees clinch the pennant against the Dodgers.

Heavyweight champion Rocky "The Rock" Marciano retired from boxing undefeated at the age of thirty-one. He won forty-nine fights; all but six of them ended in a knockout.

Records were shattered: New York Yankee Roger Maris hit his sixty-first home run against the Boston Red Sox on the final day of the 162-game season (Babe Ruth's record was 60 home runs in a 154-game season), and Philadelphia Warriors basketball player Wilt Chamberlain scored a record-setting one hundred points in one game to beat the New York Knicks 169 to 147.

You remember when Jackie Robinson broke professional baseball's color barrier, and now you saw him become the first African American inducted into the National Baseball Hall of Fame.

POP CULTURE

Owing to postwar prosperity, college enrollment increased by almost 42 percent from 1958 to 1963. If you were one of the lucky few accepted to Harvard University, tuition would have cost your parents (or you) $1,250 a year.

Cookbooks flew off the shelves: *Better Homes and Gardens Nutrition for Your Family, Casserole Cook Book, Joy of Cooking,* and *The Pillsbury Family Cook Book* were all best sellers.

There may have been a bomb shelter in the basement or backyard of your new home. Given the very real threat of nuclear war, President John F. Kennedy advised the "prudent family" to have a bomb shelter, and civil defense officials distributed twenty-two million copies of a booklet titled *The Family Fallout Shelter*.

You were most likely to name your children Michael, David, James, Robert, or John if they were boys. For girls, Mary, Susan, Linda, Debra, or Karen were most common.

Since 1936, *Joy of Cooking* has sold more than eighteen million copies.

WHEN YOU WERE
IN YOUR 30s

IN THE NEWS

The New York Times published top-secret documents that detailed US involvement in Vietnam since World War II. Outraged, President Nixon formed a team called the "plumbers unit" to stop future government leaks—this same team would later break into the Watergate Hotel.

You and one billion other viewers (roughly one-fifth of the entire world's population!) tuned in to watch Neil Armstrong's historic "one small step."

You probably also remember the gripping seven-day saga of Apollo 13—an explosion crippled the shuttle's power, oxygen, and water supply, forcing the three astronauts to find a way to return home with very limited resources.

Nearly nine million served in the war in Vietnam from 1964 to 1973, during which time more than fifty-eight thousand Americans were killed and more than three hundred thousand wounded. Everyone was touched in some way.

AMERICA SALUTES FIRST MEN ON THE MOON

ARMSTRONG COLLINS ALDRIN

APOLLO XI
JULY 1969

The birth control pill gave women the ability to plan or prevent pregnancy, and the baby boom came to an end.

EVENTS

If you purchased a new car after 1966, it came equipped with seat belts (in all seats) and shatter-resistant windshields. Consumer advocate Ralph Nader's book *Unsafe at Any Speed* played a large part in making these safety standards law.

Dr. Christiaan Barnard became a worldwide celebrity when he performed the first successful human heart transplant in Cape Town, South Africa.

Perhaps you were among the twenty million people to take Wednesday off from work to celebrate the first Earth Day. Growing national interest in the environment soon paved the way for the Clean Air and Clean Water acts.

For better or ... weird, modern science found its way into your home. From the electric styling comb (which blew warm air) to heated water beds to the reconstituted potato chips known as "Pringles" to the microwave oven ... the future had arrived!

MUSIC

When the unique sound of a Motown hit came on your car radio, you couldn't mistake it for anything else. The Detroit label launched the careers of many black musicians, including The Supremes, Marvin Gaye and, now, Stevie Wonder.

The Monkees, a fictional TV band modeled after The Beatles' early years, had several hit songs, including "Last Train to Clarksville," "I'm a Believer," and "A Little Bit Me, A Little Bit You." Following suit, The Partridge Family hit the radio with "I Think I Love You."

Revolutionary music—such as John Lennon's "Give Peace a Chance," James Brown's "Say It Loud—I'm Black and I'm Proud," or Creedence Clearwater Revival's "Fortunate Son"—both reflected and fueled the times. Perhaps Bob Dylan said it best: "Then you better start swimmin' or you'll sink like a stone, for the times they are a-changin'."

It was a time of departures and new directions: The Beatles officially broke up, and Diana Ross parted ways with The Supremes to begin her solo career.

MOVIES

Musicals were big: *My Fair Lady, A Hard Day's Night,* and *Viva Las Vegas* all hit theaters in the same year.

Walt Disney—creator (and voice) of Mickey Mouse, pioneer of the feature-length cartoon, and founder of an entertainment empire—died from lung cancer at the age of sixty-five. (Despite persistent rumors of cryonic preservation, his remains were cremated.)

To prevent your children and their friends from seeing inappropriate movies such as *Midnight Cowboy*, the Motion Picture Association of America introduced film ratings: G for general audiences, M for mature audiences, R for restricted, and X for no one under seventeen.

Perhaps *Diamonds Are Forever,* but this James Bond film marked Sean Connery's last appearance as Agent 007.

TV

Walter Cronkite may have changed your mind about the Vietnam War—his unflinching coverage and scathing commentary on the CBS Evening News influenced mainstream public opinion.

After you were inundated with cigarette ads during your childhood and teenage years, the last-ever cigarette commercial was broadcast during *The Tonight Show Starring Johnny Carson,* one minute before new legislation banning them became law.

Your black-and-white television set did not mean that you were completely behind the times—by the early 70s, only half of America watched television in color. Either way, you probably watched the Nixon vs. Humphrey debates or the last episode of *The Fugitive* (along with twenty-five million other households).

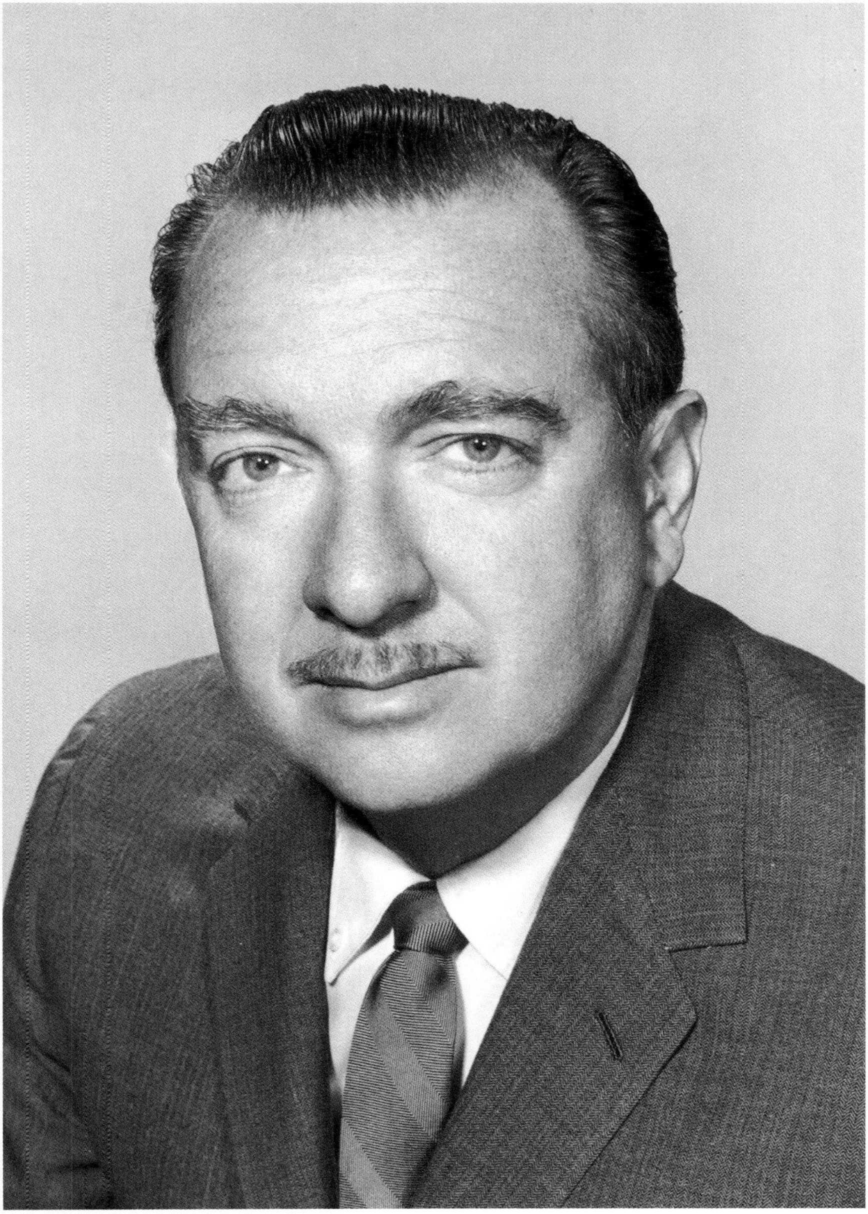

"Winning isn't everything;
it's the only thing."

VINCE LOMBARDI

SPORTS

After a celebrated career that included 536 lifetime home runs and netting American League MVP three times, Mickey Mantle announced his retirement.

Did your children learn to play tennis with a one-handed backhand? Billie Jean King's reign as the top women's tennis player may have been responsible for that.

American swimmer Mark Spitz took home seven gold medals from the 1972 Munich Olympics, setting new world records in all seven events. Thanks to satellite TV, one billion viewers watched this (and the tragic hostage crisis) live.

POP CULTURE

You could not help but notice an eclectic hippie style spreading among the youth: peace symbols, long hair, grungy jeans, fringed leather vests, miniskirts with chain belts, and granny glasses.

Also impossible to ignore was a growing movement to protest American involvement in Vietnam, unequal civil rights, and poverty.

If you moved sometime in your late thirties, a new single-family home may have cost you about $28,900. Get a promotion at work? Perhaps you financed an Audi for $3,900 or a new Rolls Royce for $29,700.

**Starbucks opened
its first coffee shop
in Seattle, Washington.**

WHEN YOU WERE
IN YOUR 40s

IN THE NEWS

Like most Americans, your confidence in the US government was shaken when President Nixon resigned rather than be impeached over the break-in at the Watergate Hotel.

One day after his inauguration, President Jimmy Carter made good on a campaign promise by extending a presidential pardon to all draft dodgers.

You and many others watched, helpless, as Iranian militants seized sixty-six American citizens and held most of them hostage at a US embassy in Tehran for more than a year.

A partial meltdown at a nuclear power plant less than ten miles from Harrisburg, PA (and one hundred miles from Washington, DC), caused nationwide panic. Three Mile Island is now cited as the location of the worst nuclear accident in American history.

Mount St. Helens erupted with a force equal to 27,000 atomic bombs, killing 57 people and sending a 16-mile-high plume of ash as far as Idaho and Montana.

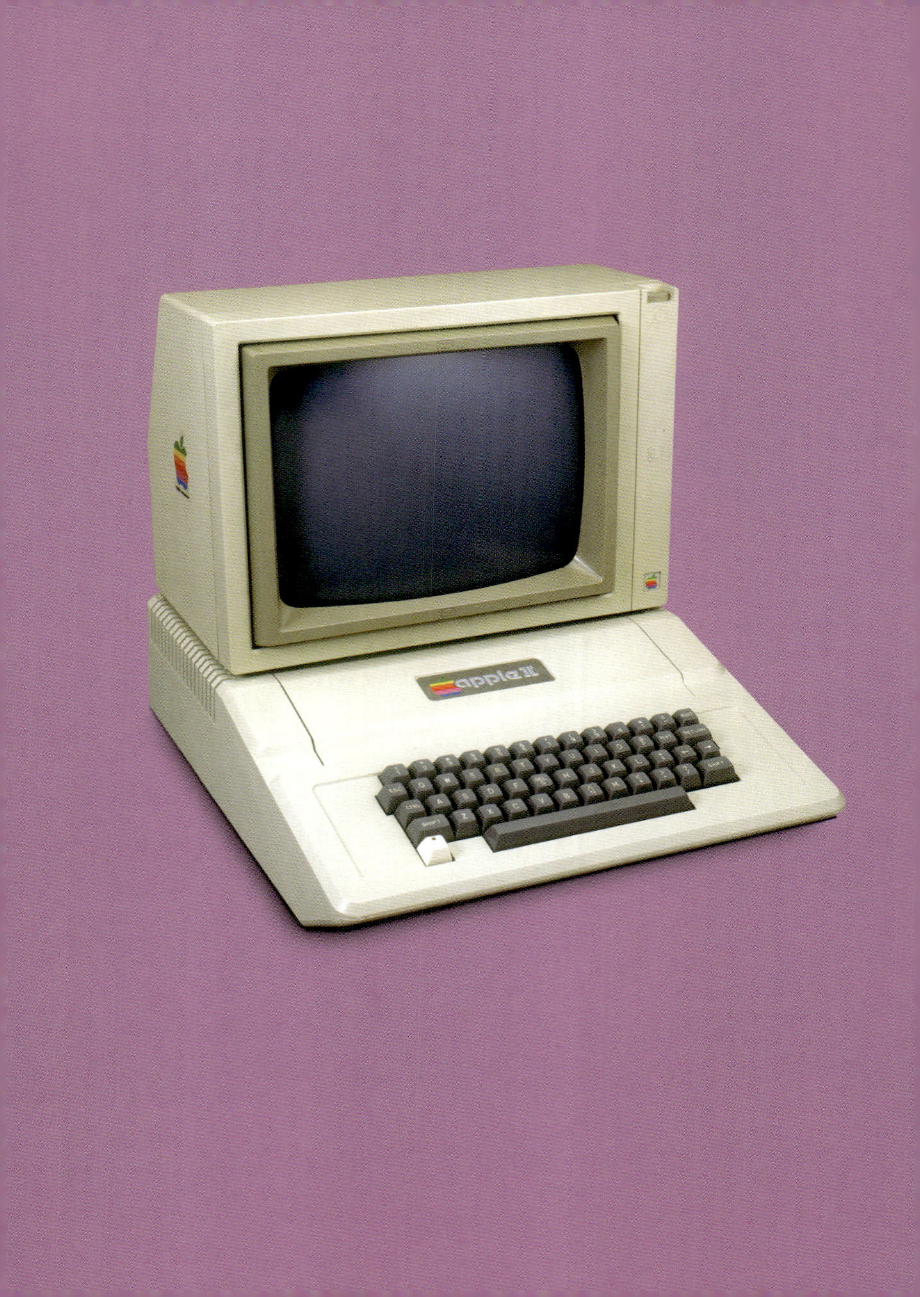
apple II

EVENTS

Technology seemed to be growing at an unchecked rate: robotic arms began to replace humans on automobile assembly lines, a CAT scan could look inside your head, a space station called Skylab was orbiting the earth, and computers started to get a lot smaller (and faster!) thanks to the microprocessor chip.

Back at home, disposable razors found their way into the bathroom (and landfills), while your new telephone answering machine was there to take a message (on very small cassette tapes).

While the rest of the country suffered from a deep recession, a growing technology boom (not to mention the nice weather) convinced many to relocate to the South and Southwest—these states saw a population increase of more than 25 percent!

The fledgling Apple company began to sell their revolutionary Apple II personal computers, based on a design that Steve Jobs and Steve Wozniak developed in their California garage.

MUSIC

George McCrae's "Rock Your Baby" and Hues Corporation's "Rock the Boat" kicked off the short-lived disco craze, a time marked by lit floors, flashing lights, and polyester.

If you saw Elvis' final tour, you were in for quite a spectacle: that white-caped suit, his martial arts moves, those sweaty scarves. Elvis died at the age of forty-two, and only one day later, heartbroken fans had purchased his records by the millions.

The rock 'n' roll of your twenties had evolved—and not quietly. Heavy metal bands Led Zeppelin, AC/DC, Aerosmith, and Van Halen blew out their amps (and your eardrums); innovative rockers The Eagles and Fleetwood Mac changed the musical landscape; and punk rockers the Sex Pistols, Patti Smith, the Velvet Underground, and the Ramones spoke directly to modern teenagers' rebellion.

If you had $900-$1,000 to burn, you may have purchased a Sony CDP-101—the world's first commercially released CD player.

Hotel California
RAMONES
LED ZEPPELIN
NEVER MIND
THE BOLLOCKS
HERE'S THE
SEX PISTOLS

"May the Force be with you."

STAR WARS

MOVIES

Science fiction and comic book fans were validated at last by blockbusters like *Superman, Close Encounters of the Third Kind, Alien, Star Trek: The Motion Picture,* and the granddaddy of them all: *Star Wars.*

Other popular movies of the time included *Grease, Jaws, Rocky, Taxi Driver, Annie Hall, Apocalypse Now,* and *Manhattan.*

You were a young teen when Mohandas Gandhi was assassinated, but Richard Attenborough's three-hour epic capably filled in the parts you probably missed. *Gandhi* swept the Academy Awards, winning nine in total, including best actor for Ben Kingsley.

Burt Reynolds, John Travolta, Clint Eastwood, Sylvester Stallone, Jane Fonda, Robert De Niro, Barbra Streisand, Dustin Hoffman, and Meryl Streep were the leading stars of the day.

TV

Saturday Night Live premiered, launching the careers of Bill Murray, Chevy Chase, Dan Aykroyd, Steve Martin, and many others.

If you watched anything other than *Roots* between January 23 and 30, 1977, then you were in the minority. An incredible 85 percent of the viewing public watched the twelve-hour miniseries adaptation of Alex Haley's novel.

Everyone loved a sitcom: *Three's Company, Laverne and Shirley, Happy Days, Mork and Mindy,* and *M*A*S*H* were all hits.

And if you enjoyed *The Mary Tyler Moore Show,* you were certainly not alone—daring for its time, the show about a single professional woman won the Emmy Award for outstanding comedy series three years in a row and launched three spin-off series!

BOSTON
SEOUL
34 MI
54 Km
CONEY ISLAND
7033
SAN FRANCISCO
259 MI
5610

"I don't want them to forget Ruth; I just want them to remember me!"

HANK AARON

SPORTS

Gymnast Nadia Comaneci of Romania became the first athlete to score a perfect ten at the Olympic games. Not bad for a fourteen-year-old!

Former Olympic champion Leon Spinks challenged Muhammad Ali for the world heavyweight title and won it in a split decision. Ali, however, regained the title seven months later.

There's a reason he was the world's top-earning tennis player by the end of the decade—Björn Borg won a record five consecutive Wimbledon men's singles championships between 1976 and 1980.

Hank Aaron beat Babe Ruth's home run record of 714 on April 8, 1974. He didn't stop there—Aaron holds a total of 755 career home runs.

POP CULTURE

Now that your kids were all out of the house, perhaps you took a long-overdue trip to Europe. International tourism to cities such as London, Venice, and Paris set new records.

You may have developed a healthy distrust of unnatural chemicals. Sales of health food products rose from $140 million in 1970 to $1.6 billion in 1979!

On the other hand, by the time you turned forty, there were nearly seven thousand fast food restaurants (compared to thirty-four hundred just a decade earlier). Is it any wonder that roughly 33 percent of meals were eaten out of the house?

The Disco Era brought flashing lights, spinning mirror balls, and polyester clothes. Perhaps you still have your favorite leisure suit in a closet somewhere?

If your children had children of their own, your grandsons might be named Michael, Christopher, Matthew, Jason, or David. Your granddaughters might be named Jennifer, Jessica, Amanda, Sarah, or Melissa.

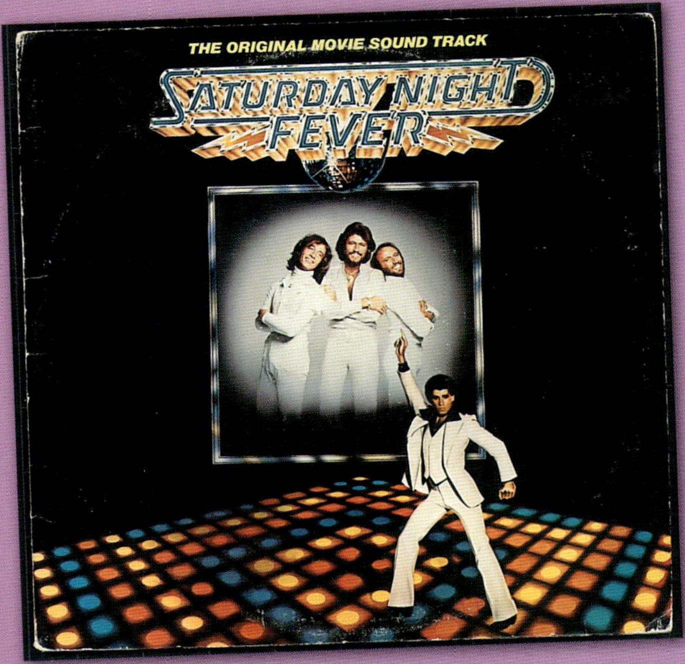
THE ORIGINAL MOVIE SOUND TRACK
SATURDAY NIGHT
FEVER

WHEN YOU WERE
IN YOUR 50s

IN THE NEWS

No one likes Mondays, but October 19, 1987, was particularly bad: after several months of record gains, the Dow Jones Industrial Average plummeted 508 points—nearly 23 percent of its total value.

Millions watched in horror as the space shuttle Challenger—whose crew included Christa McAuliffe, a school teacher—exploded moments after takeoff.

You probably still remember horrific images of wild birds covered in black oil. The Exxon Valdez, piloted by an inexperienced third mate, went off course and struck a reef in Alaska's Prince William Sound, spreading more than eleven million gallons of crude oil over thirteen hundred miles of pristine coastline.

You saw the rise of the Berlin Wall when you were in your twenties, and now you saw it fall. With it, the Cold War came to a symbolic end.

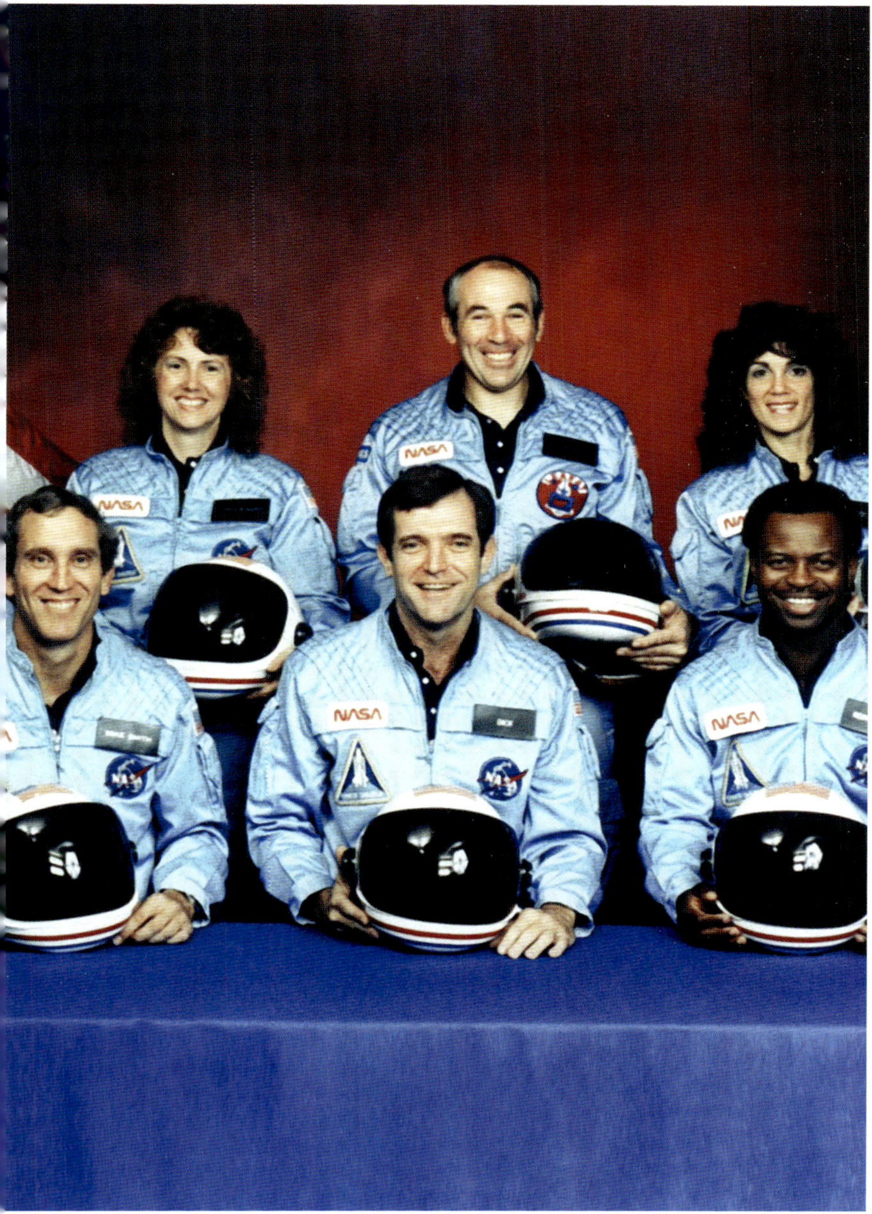

Over one million people took to the streets of New York City to join the largest antinuclear demonstration in history.

EVENTS

....

Most thought the AIDS epidemic was only a threat to homosexuals and drug addicts until thirteen-year-old Ryan White made his story known. He had acquired the virus through a blood transfusion.

The wreck of the RMS *Titanic* was at last found—broken in two and twelve thousand feet under the North Atlantic. What you didn't know was that this discovery happened during a top-secret Navy mission to find the remains of two Cold War–era nuclear submarines.

Slain civil rights leader Martin Luther King Jr. was honored with the dedication of a new national holiday. Initially, only twenty-seven states observed Martin Luther King Jr. Day.

You may have purchased a new Cometron or Comet Catcher telescope to watch the once-in-a-lifetime passing of Halley's Comet. This orbiting ball of ice and dust passes earth about once every seventy-six years, despite Pope Calixtus III excommunicating it as an agent of the devil in 1456.

MUSIC

First featured in a commercial for the California raisin industry, four singing raisins spawned four albums, two TV specials, and a host of merchandise. The shriveled superstars are now part of the Smithsonian's permanent collection.

Think the title track to Bruce Springsteen's hit album *Born in the U.S.A.* is about American pride? Many did, and still do. However, "The Boss" wrote the song about how shamefully Vietnam veterans were treated after the war ended.

Remember all the torn T-shirts and jeans? Those kids probably listened to heavy-metal bands like Bon Jovi, Guns N' Roses, Whitesnake, Poison, or Van Halen.

Other familiar hit songs include Prince's "Purple Rain," Michael Jackson's "Thriller," and Tina Turner's "What's Love Got to Do With It?" (though by now, you probably found yourself listening mostly to "oldies" stations).

MOVIES

Blockbuster popcorn flicks, such as *Raiders of the Lost Ark, Return of the Jedi, Ghostbusters, The Terminator, Back to the Future,* and especially *E.T. the Extra-Terrestrial,* reigned supreme.

Tom Cruise became a heartthrob with *Risky Business,* and *Top Gun* inspired a fashion throwback: leather bomber and aviator jackets were popular again.

Critical hits *She's Gotta Have It* and *Do the Right Thing* lifted young African-American director Spike Lee to prominence.

"Movie night" didn't always mean going to the theater—all you had to do was rent a VHS tape from the local Ritz Video or Movie Gallery and pop it into your VCR. (Just don't forget to rewind!)

TV

At a time when the sitcom was not popular and no successful show featured a black family, the runaway success of *The Cosby Show* was a bit of a surprise. It was the third most popular show in its first year and the most popular show for the next four.

Why go to the mall? The Home Shopping Network gave you the ability to make all of your impulse purchases from the comfort of your home.

The final episode of *M*A*S*H* shattered TV records by drawing nearly 106 million viewers. It held this record for twenty-seven years—until 2010's *Super Bowl XLIV*.

Harkening back to the days of old-time radio, soap operas—such as *Dallas, Dynasty, Knots Landing,* and *Falcon Crest*—were suddenly appointment viewing. An estimated two-thirds of all women with access to television watched at least one soap a day.

> "There's 57 channels and nothing on."

BRUCE SPRINGSTEEN

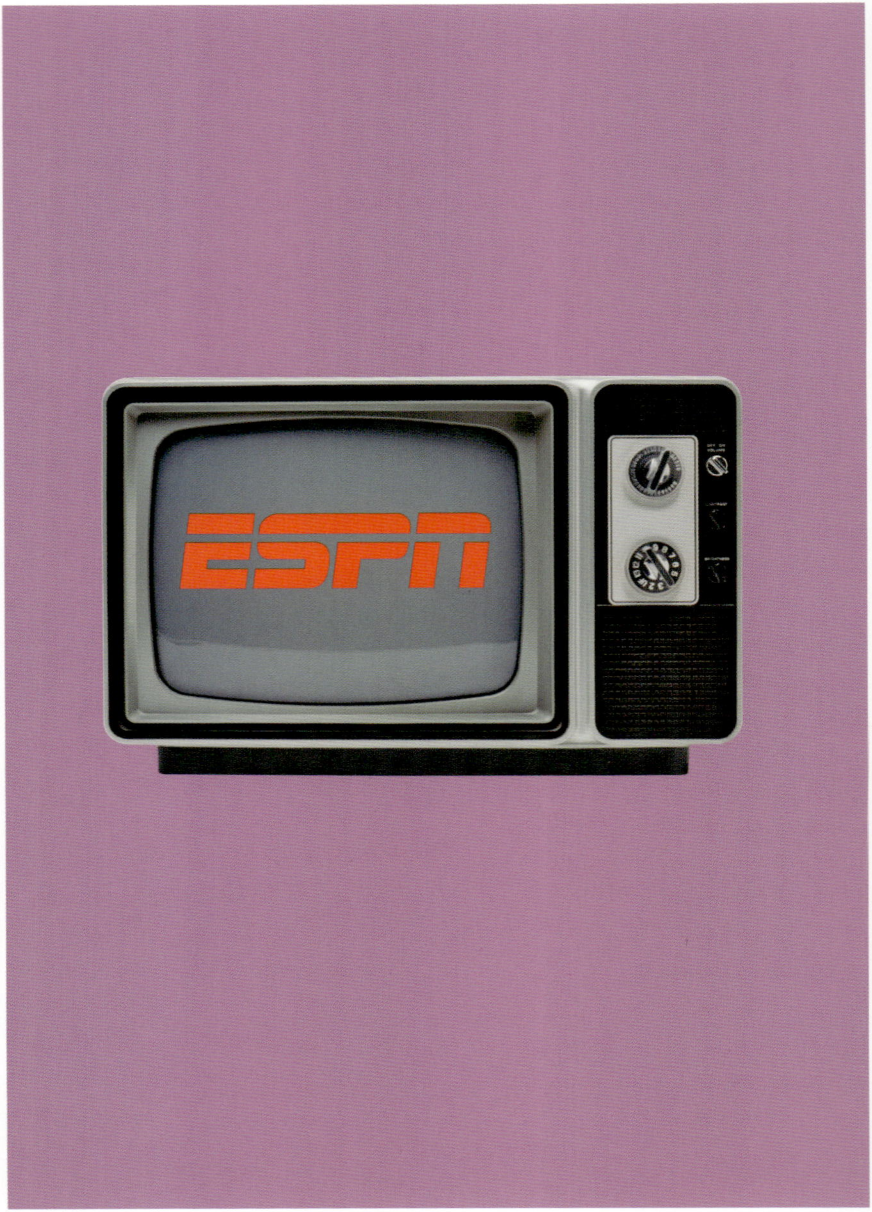
ESPN

SPORTS

If it hadn't yet, the widespread cocaine problem in the mid-80s got your attention when it claimed two athletes: Len Bias, newly drafted by the Boston Celtics, and professional football player Don Rogers.

Before his illegal betting got him ousted from baseball, Cincinnati Reds batter Pete Rose surpassed 4,191 hits to break a record set fifty-seven years earlier by Ty Cobb.

By 1987, nearly 50 percent of American homes had cable TV. And the most popular cable channel by far was ESPN, with sixty million subscribers by the end of the decade.

There were plans to install lights in Wrigley Field when you were a kid, but the owner decided instead to donate the materials to the war effort. Now, for the first time since the ballpark opened in 1914, there were lights in Wrigley.

POP CULTURE

The private lives of celebrities were suddenly matters of great interest. Supermarket tabloids—such as *Star, the Globe,* and *the National Enquirer*—sold by the tens of millions.

It's all about you! Self-help books, from *You Can Negotiate Anything* to *Be Happy You Are Loved,* began to fly off the shelves.

Trivial Pursuit was the hot new game, plastic flowers danced to music, New Coke was quickly replaced with Coca-Cola Classic, and Cabbage Patch Kids were a huge craze.

The savings-and-loan crisis may have made it difficult for your children to acquire financing for their first homes.

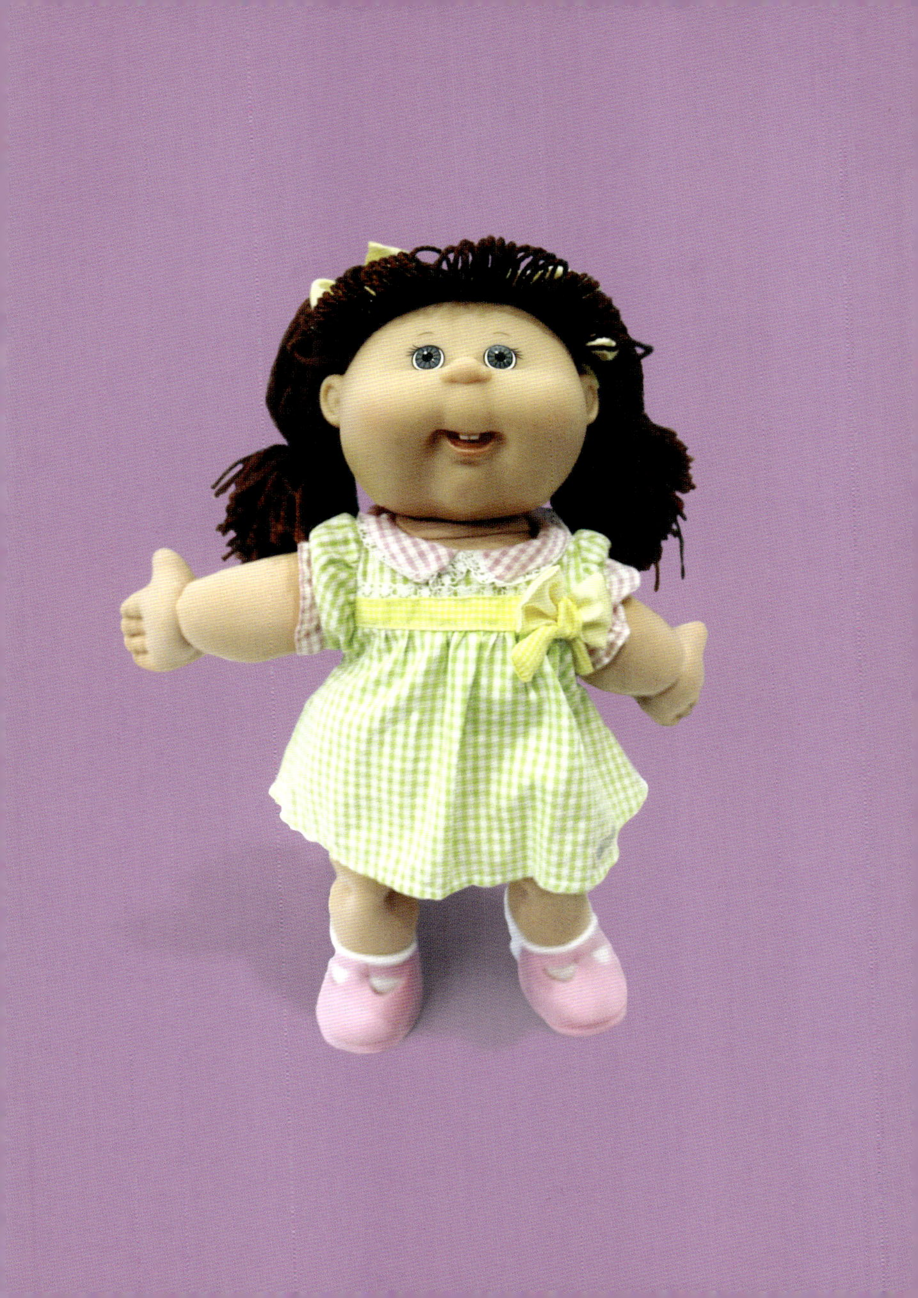

WHEN YOU WERE
IN YOUR 60s

IN THE NEWS

A historic peace agreement in Northern Ireland promised to end the terrorism and civil unrest that had plagued the region for more than eight decades.

Bill Clinton was the first president born after World War II and also the first Democrat to win reelection since FDR in 1944.

Harkening back to the *Chicago Tribune*'s gaffe during your teenage years, many news stations prematurely reported Vice President Al Gore the winner of the 2000 presidential election.

September 11, 2001. We will never forget.

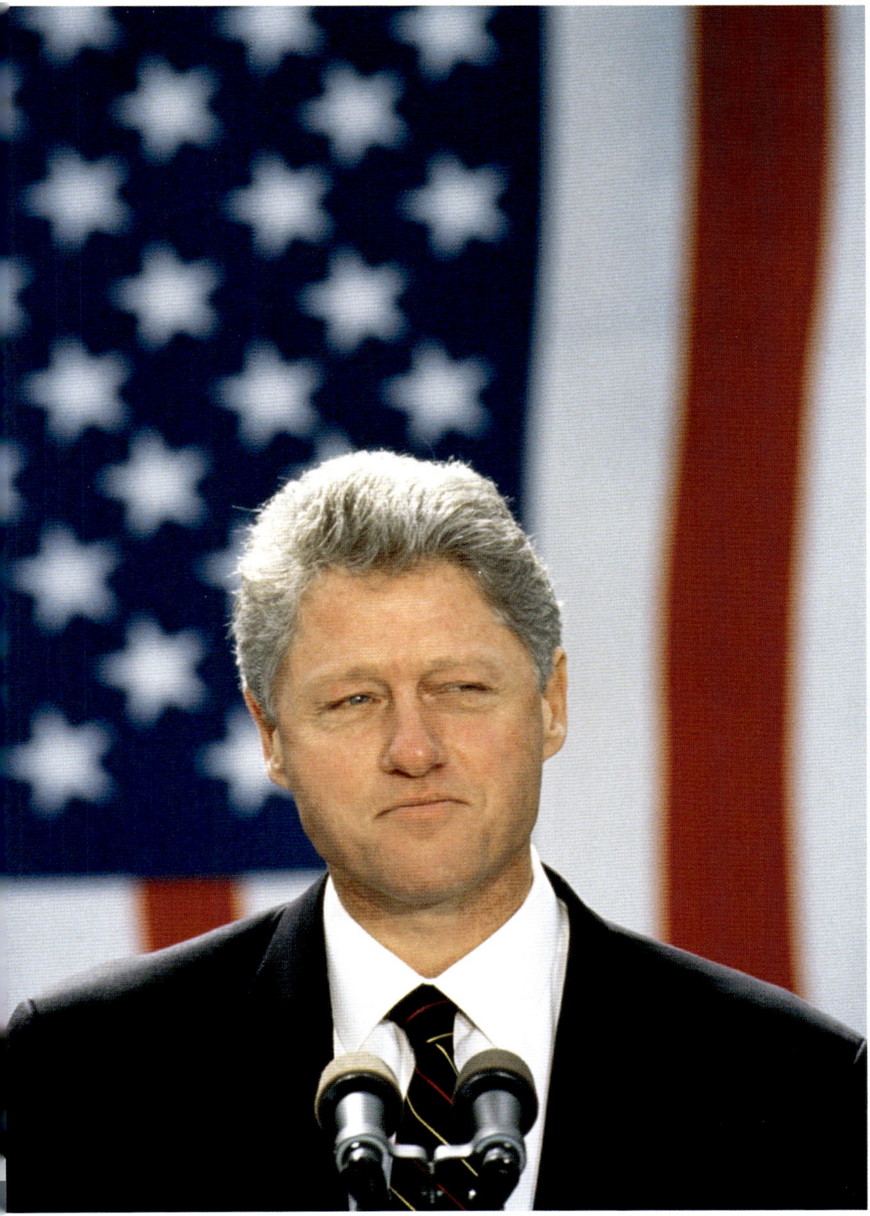

Y2K

EVENTS

Your science fiction dreams (or fears) came true when scientists in Scotland successfully cloned a lamb named Dolly, igniting a worldwide debate about the implications of cloning technology.

Genetic modification allowed farmers to begin growing produce that was larger and more resistant to insecticides, though some scientists worried about the effects that these altered crops could have on the environment.

If you hadn't gotten around to learning how to use a computer, you had even less incentive to do so now: the Y2K bug threatened to send society back to the 1900s by exploiting an oversight in computers' internal clocks.

Previously a bulky thing for affluent people (or show-offs), the cell phone evolved by leaps and bounds.

MUSIC

Elton John rewrote a song that was originally about Marilyn Monroe and performed it at the funeral of Princess Diana. "Candle in the Wind 1997" quickly sold thirty-four million copies, and all proceeds were donated to charity.

Whitney Houston made her big-screen debut with Kevin Costner in *The Bodyguard*, and the album (which featured her international chart-topping cover of Dolly Parton's "I Will Always Love You") became the best-selling soundtrack of all time.

Whether or not you listened to them, Los Del Rio's "Macarena," Celine Dion's "My Heart Will Go On," and Ricky Martin's "Livin' La Vida Loca" were on the radio quite a lot.

KEVIN COSTNER
WHITNEY HOUSTON
THE BODYGUARD
ORIGINAL SOUNDTRACK ALBUM

"Life is like a box of chocolates."

FORREST GUMP

MOVIES

Everything old was new again. Movies based on the radio and television shows of your youth included *Dennis the Menace, The Shadow,* and *Leave It to Beaver.*

You probably also enjoyed *Thelma and Louise, The Piano,* and the heartrending *Schindler's List,* which earned six Oscars, including best director and best picture.

Seabiscuit, starring Tobey Maguire and Jeff Bridges, chronicled the life story of a familiar underdog hero from your childhood years and was nominated for seven Academy Awards.

TV

Millions watched minute-by-minute televised coverage of scandals—from the OJ Simpson police chase and trial to the Tonya Harding–Nancy Kerrigan assault to charges of infidelity on the part of the president.

Even if you were one of very few people who didn't watch *Seinfeld*, you couldn't escape people quoting it (not that there's anything wrong with that). After nine seasons, more than thirty million people tuned in to watch the series finale.

You may have watched *Candid Camera* with Alan Funt, but megapopular shows such as *Survivor* and *American Idol* seemed to bear little resemblance to the reality TV of your twenties.

Nearly 60 percent of Americans spent most evenings on the couch, giving rise to the term "couch potato."

"Married men live longer than single men. But married men are a lot more willing to die."

JOHNNY CARSON

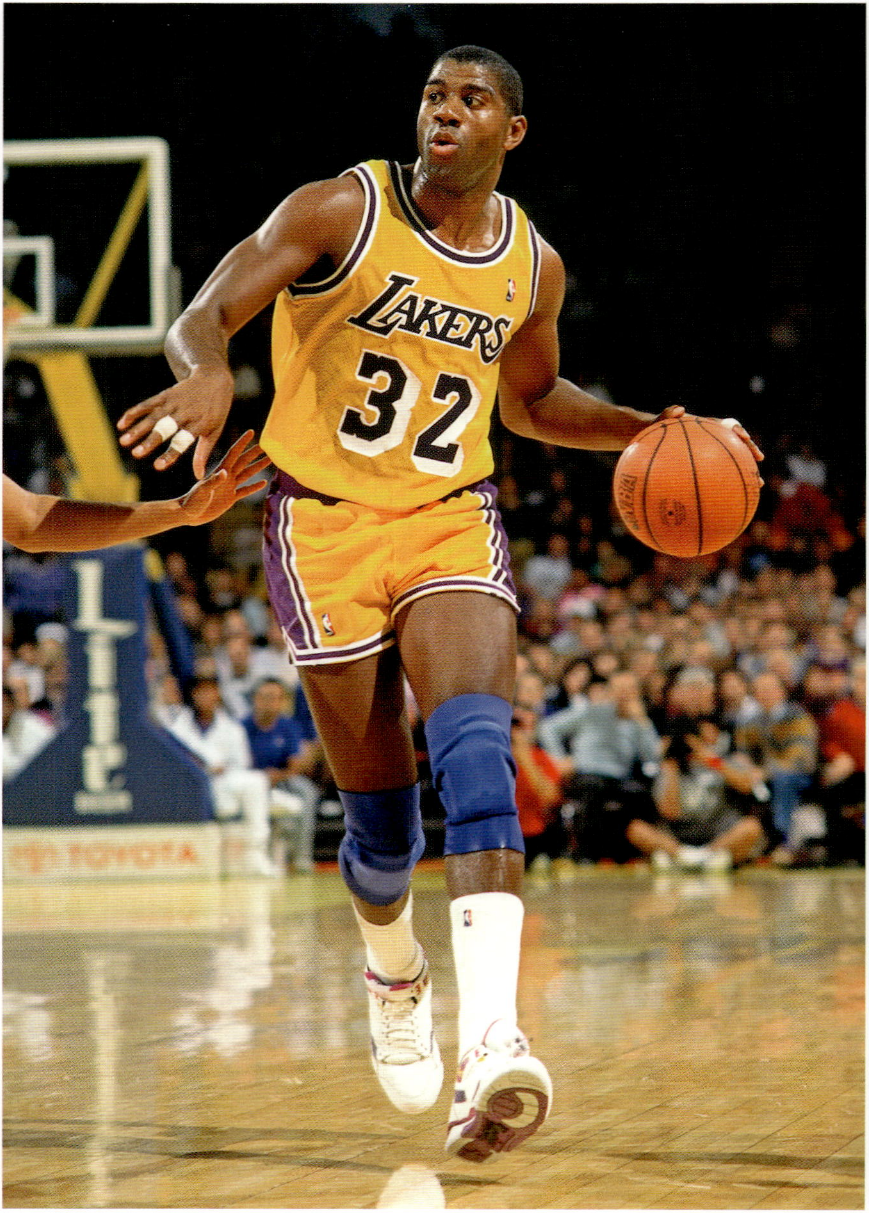
LAKERS
32
TOYOTA

SPORTS

Twenty years after losing boxing's world heavyweight title to Muhammad Ali (and after ten years away from heavyweight competitions), George Foreman reclaimed his title by knocking out Michael Moorer in ten rounds.

Basketball fans were stunned when three-time MVP Earvin "Magic" Johnson announced that he was HIV-positive and would retire from the NBA.

Baseball fans were not pleased when a 257-day strike led to the cancellation of that year's World Series.

At twenty-one, Tiger Woods became the youngest golfer to win the Masters Tournament—and by a record twelve strokes.

POP CULTURE

Ah, retirement. The Social Security Act was passed around the time you were born, and a good thing, too! But just because you didn't have to get up for work anymore didn't mean you stayed home. Through volunteering and staying active in the community, retirees were starting a "new chapter" in increasing numbers.

Fanny packs were hip, emoticons put smiles in your e-mail, Beanie Babies were must-have collectibles, books on tape let you read while driving, and you learned that *Men Are From Mars, Women Are From Venus.*

Dr. Deepak Chopra may have changed your mind about alternative medicine with his best-selling book *Ageless Body, Timeless Mind.* If so, you weren't alone—*Time* magazine even named Chopra one of the top one hundred icons and heroes of the century.

You weren't imagining it: Popular culture seemed obsessed with youth as advertisers trained their sights almost exclusively on your grandchildren and their friends. By the late 90s, teens were thirty-one million strong and willing to spend most of their money on music and movies.

> "Men are from Mars, women are from Venus."

AUTHOR JOHN GRAY

WHEN YOU WERE
IN YOUR 70s

IN THE NEWS

No one expected the devastation of Hurricane Katrina. The Category Three storm claimed the lives of over thirteen hundred New Orleans natives and the homes of many more.

The space shuttle Columbia unexpectedly disintegrated after its return from a successful sixteen-day mission. All seven astronauts were killed, and debris from the shuttle rained across hundreds of miles of Texas countryside.

From Mr. Universe to the Terminator to . . . California's thirty-eighth governor? After surprising the world by announcing his candidacy on *The Tonight Show with Jay Leno,* voters elected Arnold Schwarzenegger over 134 other candidates.

When you heard the news, you probably thought it was a practical joke: Pluto is no longer considered a planet.

Facebook is launched, and later becomes the most popular social networking site on the Web, with over one billion users.

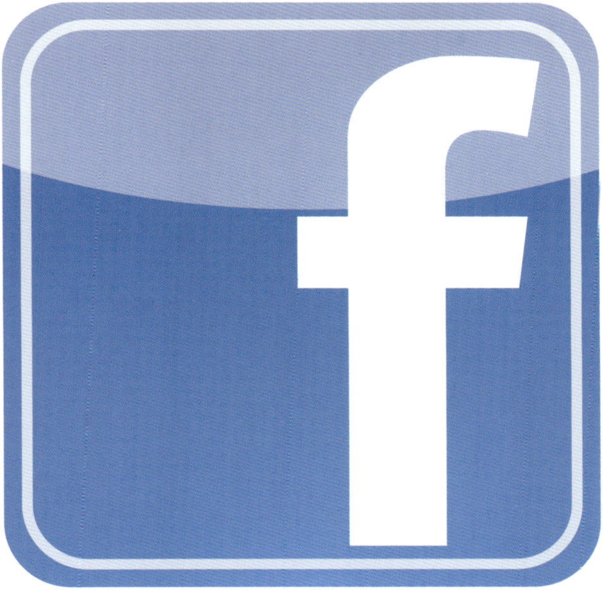

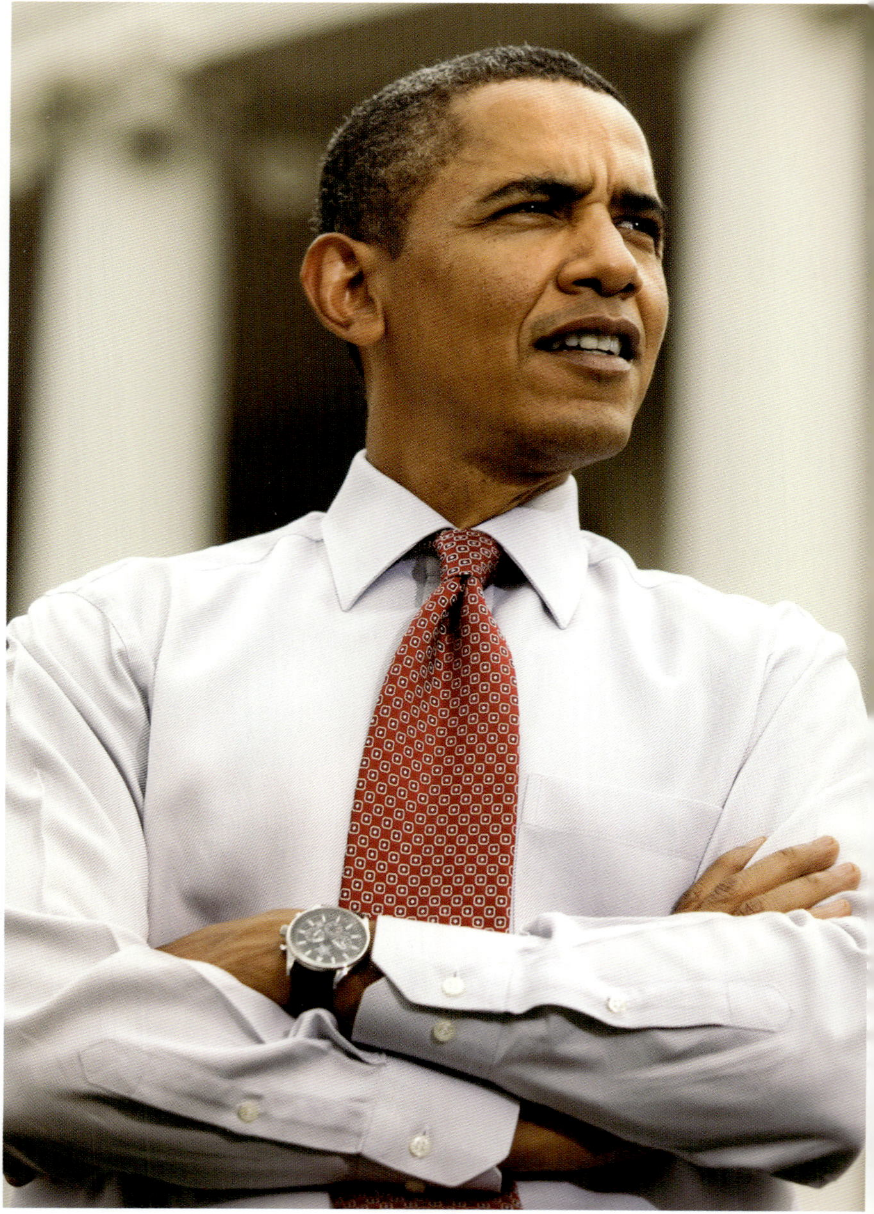

EVENTS

A massive earthquake measuring 9.0 on the Richter scale loosed a disastrous tsunami on Southeast Asia, killing over 225,000 and displacing 1.2 million more.

Iceland's Eyjafjallajökull volcano erupted for the first time since 1821, sending a plume of volcanic ash thirty thousand feet into the air and grounding airplanes from the United Kingdom to Russia for six days.

An explosion on an oil rig fifty miles off the coast of Louisiana killed eleven workers and eventually resulted in the worst oil spill in US history—an estimated 172 million gallons of crude permeated the Gulf Coast, a disaster fifteen times greater than that of the Exxon Valdez.

From humble beginnings to 44th president of the United States, Barack Obama showed the world that the American dream is very much alive.

MUSIC

The way people listen to music has changed just as much as the music itself: from LPs to 8-tracks and then cassette tapes to CDs and finally to portable MP3 players like the Apple iPod, which can easily hold your entire music library.

Alicia Keys was a piano-playing phenomenon, releasing four albums (including her runaway sophomore hit, *The Diary of Alicia Keys*) and stacking up twelve Grammy Awards.

The world was stunned to learn that Michael Jackson died of a drug overdose less than a month before his sold-out concerts in London.

Coming full circle from the days of radio, online radio-streaming services like Pandora gave anyone the ability to play a personalized selection of music through their computer.

WHEN YOU WERE IN YOUR 70s

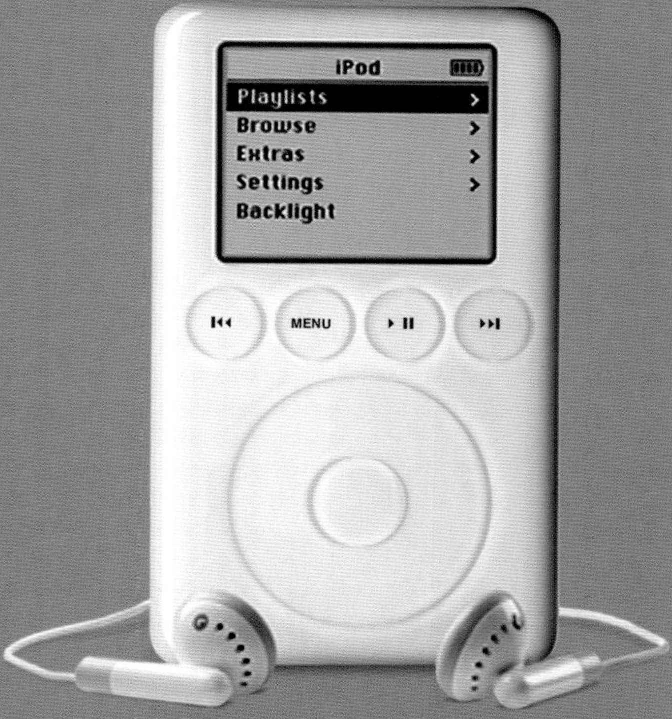
iPod
Playlists
Browse
Extras
Settings
Backlight
MENU

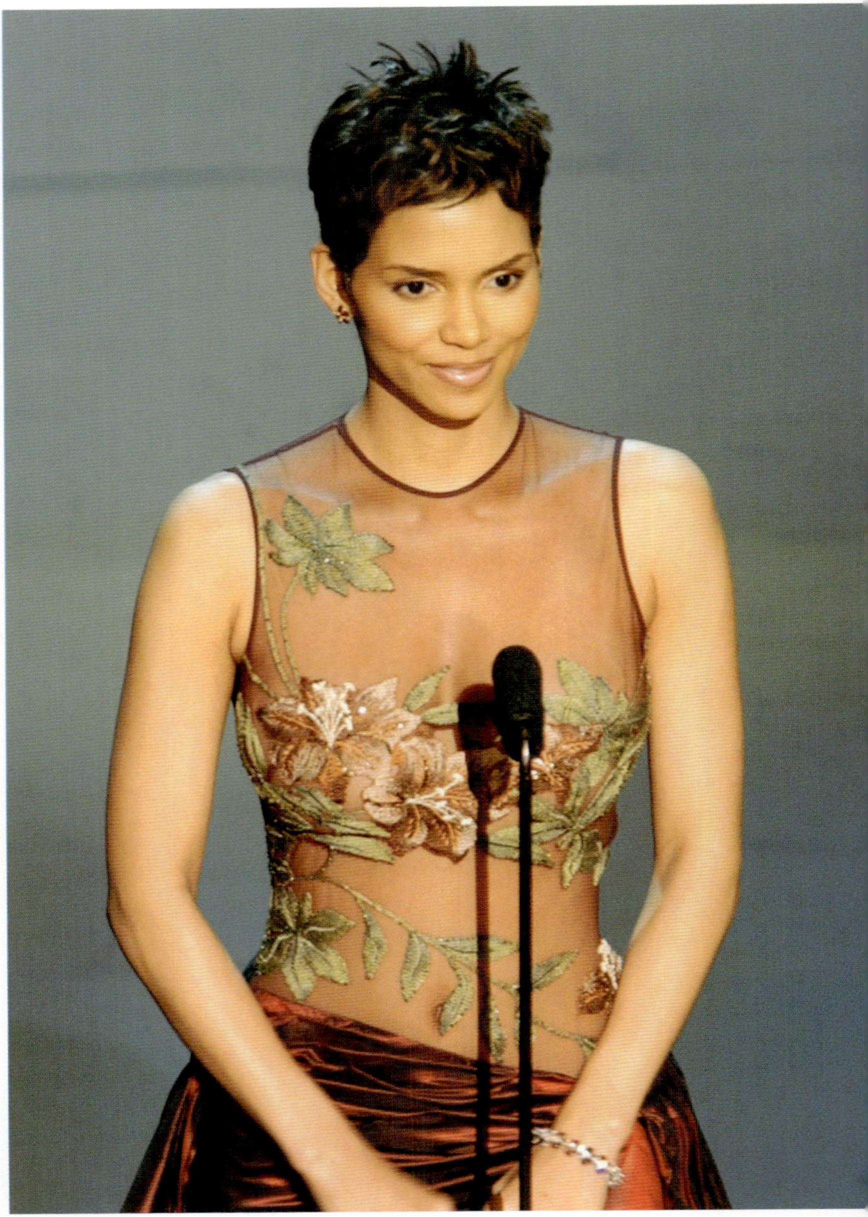

MOVIES

Good Night, and Good Luck portrayed the McCarthyism of your twenties through the eyes of Edward R. Murrow and his producer Fred W. Friendly.

Academy Award-winning *Dreamgirls* may have seemed familiar to you—the story closely mirrored that of Diana Ross and The Supremes.

Superhero movies, many featuring characters that first debuted in comic books you may have read as a child, were everywhere! (And, by the way, if you still have those books they're probably worth a few dollars ...)

Thanks to her powerful performance in *Monster's Ball*, Halle Berry became the first African-American woman to win an Academy Award for best actress.

TV

Remember when the first television sets were built into really heavy, wooden cabinets? Flat-screen TVs are so light that they can be mounted on your wall.

You had to spring for the premium cable package (or wait for the DVDs) to catch some of the best shows on television, such as *The Sopranos, Six Feet Under, The Wire, The Shield,* and one that is certain to bring back some memories—*Mad Men.*

If you watched CNN's coverage of the 2008 presidential elections, you may have seen something right out of the science fiction movies of the drive-in days: a live holographic image of a reporter from Chicago beamed into a studio in New York.

Now you can watch TV shows on your computer!

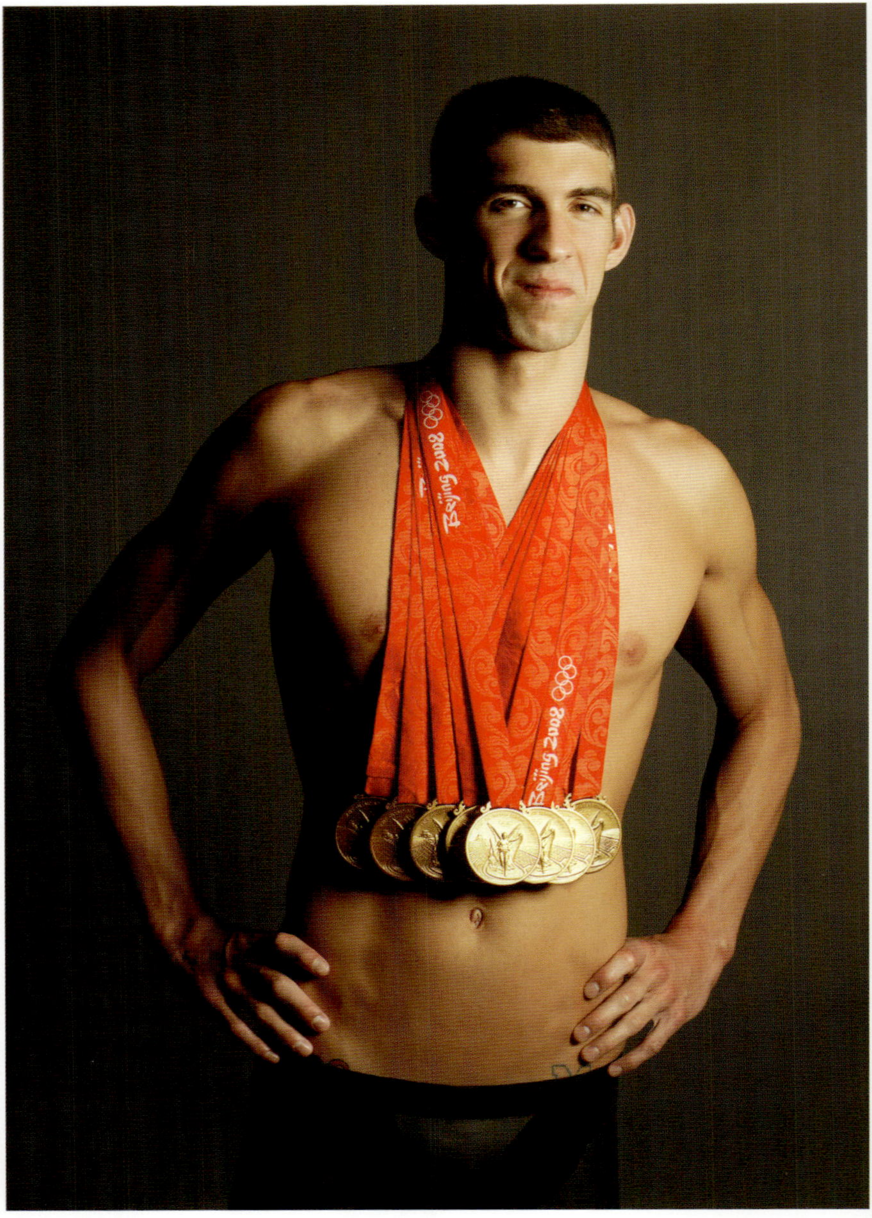
Beijing 2008
Beijing 2008

SPORTS

• •

Long-beleaguered Boston Red Sox fans had their day when their team beat the St. Louis Cardinals to win their first World Series Championship in eighty-six years.

The issue of steroid abuse in professional baseball came to public attention when former player Jose Canseco published a controversial memoir titled *Juiced: Wild Times, Rampant 'Roids, Smash Hits, and How Baseball Got Big*.

American swimmer Michael Phelps won eight events at the 2008 Beijing Olympics, setting a new record for the most gold medals won in a single Olympics.

American cyclist Lance Armstrong survived cancer to take home seven Tour de France titles—only to have all of them stripped away after allegations of performance-enhancing drug use surfaced.

POP CULTURE

Contemporary fashion has taken a cue from previous decades—"vintage" items such as cocktail and sheath dresses, as well as men's blazers, have become popular with today's youth. (Could it be that they *do* listen to their elders?)

Joan Rivers is older than you, but she looks like she could be your much younger cousin. Quick fixes to looking youthful are more popular than ever. Botox injections, which temporarily paralyze certain facial muscles, smoothing wrinkles and creating a more youthful (if somewhat puffy) face, are all the rage.

While many things have changed since the days of your youth, much has not. For instance, a quick look at the shelves of your local grocery store will reveal Ritz Crackers, Eight O'Clock Coffee, Morton Salt, French's Mustard, Campbell's Tomato Soup, and Spam—all products that have been around since you were a kid!

If your grandchildren have become parents, they most likely named your great-grandsons Jacob, Ethan, Michael, Joshua, or Alexander. Your great-granddaughters may be named Emily, Isabella, Emma, Olivia, or Ava.

"I've had so much plastic surgery, when I die they'll donate my body to Tupperware."

JOAN RIVERS

NOW

MOST PEOPLE YOUR AGE ARE:

- Currently married and suburban homeowners.
- Retired but spending their time being active.
- Socializing in the community, e-mailing family and friends, volunteering or working part-time, and spending time on hobbies such as gardening and home repair.
- Curious about new technology.
- More educated than their parents were.
- Worried about outliving their assets but more financially secure than any other generation alive today.
- Likely to vote Republican.
- Still learning!

LOOK WHO ELSE IS IN THEIR 80s:

- Willie Nelson, musician
- Cormac McCarthy, novelist and playwright
- Alan Arkin, actor
- Ruth Bader Ginsburg, Supreme Court Justice
- Larry King, television and radio host
- Jane Goodall, primatologist
- Gene Wilder, actor
- Ralph Nader, political activist
- Joan Rivers, television personality
- Hank Aaron, baseball right fielder
- Tenzin Gyatso, the fourteenth Dalai Lama
- Jerry Lee Lewis, musician
- Yoko Ono, artist and activist
- Gloria Steinem, feminist spokeswoman
- Ron Paul, politician
- Giorgio Armani, fashion designer
- Dame Judi Dench, actress

IF YOU HAVE ENJOYED THIS BOOK, WE WOULD LOVE TO HEAR FROM YOU.

Please send your comments to:
Hallmark Book Feedback
P.O. Box 419034
Mail Drop 215
Kansas City, MO 64141

Or e-mail us at:
booknotes@hallmark.com